T HERE IS A TW  control and a state that threate... that defends Americans' liberty. C. S. Lewis described this peculiarly modern threat in an introduction to the 1961 edition of *The Screwtape Letters*: *"The greatest evil is not done now in those sordid 'dens of crime' that Dickens loved to paint. It is not even done in concentration camps and labor camps. In those we see its final result. But it is conceived and ordered (moved, seconded, carried and minuted) in clear, carpeted, warmed and well-lighted offices, by quiet men with white collars and cut fingernails and smooth-shaven cheeks who do not need to raise their voice."*

On the night in 1972 when Richard Nixon won a landslide presidential reelection, the then-Governor of California and future president Ronald Reagan told United Press International, "There is evidence of a developing philosophy in the United States against the growth of big government, costs and influence. I think many Democrats had second thoughts in the direction that the country was going and decided it was the wrong way. Mr. Nixon is a man who wants to decentralize federal power and I think that most of the country agrees with that philosophy."

Echoing this in his inaugural address in 2017, President Donald Trump declared, "we are transferring power from Washington, D.C. and giving it back to you, the American People. For too long, a small group in our nation's Capital has reaped the rewards of government while the people have borne the cost. Washington flourished – but the people did not share in its wealth. Politicians prospered – but the jobs left, and the factories closed. The establishment protected itself, but not the citizens of our country. Their victories have not been your victories; their triumphs have not been your triumphs; and while they celebrated in our nation's Capital, there was little to celebrate for struggling families all across our land."

While the president's critics reflect with intoxicated self-satisfaction on the sound and

> *By every measure of personal and national prosperity, the United States is better off now than it was before Donald Trump was elected.*

fury of "The Resistance," the president and his supporters have won some durable political victories despite unyielding opposition. By every measure of personal and national prosperity, the United States is better off now than it was before Donald Trump was elected. Gone is the lofty sounding rhetoric of globalism that led to unwinnable foreign wars and open borders. Back is talk of how government can serve the people and what we can do together as Americans.

But you'd hardly be able to learn of his accomplishments by watching cable news. These allegedly non-partisan organs of the press continue indulging their perverse obsessions with Russian conspiracy theories, West Wing intrigue, and the president's Twitter feed. It's exhausting – and also largely beside the point.

Also conspicuous in the commentary surrounding the Trump administration are the dogs that haven't barked. These are the predictions of imminent calamity certain to accompany a Trump presidency that have, happily, failed to materialize. For one, nuclear war has not broken out, despite this being one of Trump detractors' favorite predictions. Nor has the president sold the country down the river to Vladimir Putin; he hasn't ignored court orders, hasn't shut down the free press, and hasn't fired Robert Mueller. Of course, Mueller's perfidy may yet demand action.

After more than a year of peace and prosperity, more people are likely to believe that such outlandish predictions tell us less about the president and more about the temperament of his critics. Hillary Clinton and Jill Stein went into federal court immediately after the 2016 election alleging vote tampering.

Their suits were promptly dismissed, often in withering decisions from the judges, for lack of evidence. There was, however, evidence of Democrat voter fraud in places like the Detroit precincts that went heavily for Hillary – so heavily in fact that there were more votes cast than there were registered voters. The Russia "collusion" story keeps changing because it is a hoax. But the Russia narrative isn't really about Russia or even about Donald Trump. It's about relitigating the 2016 election. It's about the permanent political class defending its power and prerogatives by any means necessary.

Despite the sustained assault from enemies far and wide determined to render his election moot, President Trump is governing. His supporters often cite achievements like Neil Gorsuch and a raft of solid judicial appointments, tax reform, and the enforcement of immigration laws. More subtle observers note that Trump has confronted the stifling anti-rational orthodoxy of political correctness, with Trump usually coming out the winner. And of course there's the signal victory evident even to his fiercest critics: he's not Hillary Clinton.

Behind the scenes, the president is reducing regulation, shrinking the deep state, and enlarging the role of the citizen. As the English philosopher and critic of the French Enlightenment Nick Land explains, "From Thomas Hobbes to Hans-Hermann Hoppe and beyond, [concerned citizens ask]: How can the sovereign power be prevented – or at least dissuaded – from devouring society?" It's a good question. In fact, it's the question behind every critique offered and fear harbored of the deep state.

Trump's pushback against the stultifying political correctness that chills free expression and thereby undermines the foundation of free government is part of these efforts and is a precondition for any permanent reduction in the size of the state. We must first be able to name a problem before we can expect to solve it. His other successes have been catalogued, celebrated, and huzzahed elsewhere.

And, well, should they be. They represent very real triumphs by the Trump administration on behalf of a citizenry that has been harassed, hectored, and oppressed by a growing, omnivorous leviathan state. If we have not quite had our substance eaten out, it's not for the government's lack of trying.

For years, Republican voters were promised constitutionalist judges, fiscal probity, and immigration enforcement. We got John "Obamacare" Roberts, runaway deficits, de facto open borders, and multiple tries at Gang of Eight amnesty. If that wasn't enough, we were led into a series of misguided wars by a

---

The Gordian knot of modern government is the leviathan state. Trump, like Alexander, has a solution: don't try and untie it, just take a big whack at it.

---

small but determined foreign policy claque focused on implementing a policy of moral imperialism that runs counter to America's history and values.

Against this butcher's bill of failures and broken promises, it is instructive to compare Donald Trump's first year in office. Unemployment is low, the stock market is high, and wages are rising. Average Americans have more money in their pockets as a result of lower taxes. (Nancy Pelosi naturally denigrated this as "crumbs.") Illegal immigration has declined, Obamacare's individual mandate is dead, and a slate of constitutionalist judges has been approved – with more on the way. These are all good things, but the Gordian knot of modern government is the leviathan state. Trump, like Alexander, has a solution: don't try and untie it, just take a big whack at it.

A HATCHET FOR REGULATION

Less than two weeks into his administration, Trump signed Executive Order 13771, requiring two regulations to be retired for every new one implemented. This was much reported on at the time, but faded quickly as the nation's journalists wrote breathless stories about the president's tweets and the first lady's shoes. But Trump's appointees used the Order as a mandate for action. The EPA's Scott Pruitt and the FDA's Scott Gottlieb deserve special recognition for energetically executing both the letter and the spirit of the law.

One of the grievances listed in the Declaration of Independence against the British was that King George had "erected a multitude of New Offices, and sent hither swarms of Officers to harass our people, and eat out their substance." Sound familiar? The federal government long ago burst its constitutional boundaries, empowered by an imperial judiciary that, starting with the New Deal Court in the 1930s and reaching its apex in 1984's *Chevron* decision, gave moral and legal cover to the anti-constitutional growth of the administrative state.

Limited-government conservatives and libertarians have decried the growth of the state for decades, believing that it is both unconstitutional and, more importantly, that it is antithetical to human liberty. Ronald Reagan was the most successful political apostle of this view in the twentieth century. Yet, while he was efficacious in reintroducing this view a few generations after the New Deal broke the old constitutional order, he was unable to stem the rising tide of government expansion while in office. Opposed as much by key members of his own party as by Democrats, Reagan's efforts to curtail the growth of the administrative state were mostly stymied. Recall that it was Republican senators, swept into the majority on Reagan's coattails, that scuttled Reagan's attempt to shutter the then-three-year-old Department of Education. And rather than closing either the Department of Education or Energy, as he had promised during the campaign, Reagan created a new cabinet-level department by elevating via executive order the old Veteran's Administration created in 1930 to the Department of Veteran's Affairs.

Not only was Reagan unable to reduce the size and scope of the leviathan state, it dramatically grew on his watch. For just a few markers, look at entitlement spending, which went from $197 billion in 1981 to $497 billion in 1987. Or the national debt, which nearly trebled under Reagan from $908 billion in 1981 to a bit over $2.6 trillion in 1988. Ah, the good old days.

This is not to lay all of the blame at the feet of Reagan. Recall that Democrats controlled the House of Representatives for all eight years of his presidency, and the Senate for four of the eight. And, it must be remembered, that Reagan was busy winning the Cold War. At the time, there was still some sense that the federal government should stay within its constitutional boundaries. But as we have learned in the intervening years, the ratchet only moves in one direction. The trend, vigorously sought by the Left and timidly accepted by much of the Right, is towards ever bigger, more intrusive government.

Perhaps cognizant of Reagan's defeats or,

more likely, just predisposed for swift action, President Trump moved quickly upon taking office. Themes of citizenship and of government working for the American people, not ruling, regulating, or crowding them out of society, were central to Trump's campaign. There were four crucial pillars built on that foundation:

1. A pro-citizen immigration policy (Americans are dreamers too!).

2. An America-first foreign policy that seeks to end the era of moral imperialism that views the State Department as a colonial office that runs the world and the Defense Department as its enforcer in an ongoing series of colonial wars.

3. Pro-worker trade and economic policy.

4. Disenfranchising the deep state and returning power to the American people acting in their constitutional majority, known in the vernacular as "draining the swamp."

But Trump faces even stronger headwinds than the Reagan administration did, because of the Supreme Court's Reagan-era *Chevron* decision. In *Chevron v. Natural Resources Defense Council*, the environmentalists lost the battle

Everyone has some direct experience with the anonymous, arbitrary, capricious power of the administrative state. And it is rarely pleasant.

(Chevron prevailed in the specific issue at stake in the case) but won the war. The case enshrined the principle of judicial deference to the lawmaking power of the bureaucracy – a policy which has become the central source of the deep state's power to run the lives of Americans without their consent.

For example, in 2016 Congress passed 214 bills that have become law, compared with

3,853 rules made by the unelected, unaccountable bureaucrats who really run the country. What's worse is that these same agencies that make the rules we live by, accountable to no one, are also judge, jury, and executioner in their enforcement. They have their own enforcement arms and their own internal judicial systems. Run afoul of a rule made by the EPA or the FDA and you will be investigated by an EPA or FDA investigator and tried by an EPA or FDA administrative law "judge." If you don't like the outcome you can appeal – to the administrator of the agency. In other words, these agencies are a power unto themselves.

This trend has not gone unnoticed by the American public. A March 2018 poll conducted by Monmouth University found that 74% of Americans believe that the deep state exists and "secretly manipulate(s) or direct(s) national policy." Significantly, the polls found that "Belief in the probable existence of a deep state comes from more than 7-in-10 Americans in each partisan group." It's no wonder that Trump's promise to "drain the swamp" struck such a chord with voters and that it played well with both Republicans and Democrats.

Everyone has some direct experience with the anonymous, arbitrary, capricious power of the administrative state. And it is rarely pleasant.

That's why Trump's Executive Order 13771 is so important. The two-for-one rule it imposes on the bureaucracy mandates a material reduction in regulation. The Order provides [emphasis added]:

SECTION 1. Purpose. It is the policy of the executive branch to be prudent and financially responsible in the expenditure of funds, from both public and private sources. In addition to the management of the direct expenditure of taxpayer dollars through the budgeting process, *it is essential to manage the costs associated with the governmental imposition of private expenditures required to comply with Federal regulations.* Toward that end, it is important that for every one new regulation issued, at least two prior regulations be identified for elimination, and that the cost of planned regulations be prudently managed and controlled through a budgeting process.

Sec. 2. Regulatory Cap for Fiscal Year 2017. (a) Unless prohibited by law, whenever an executive department or agency (agency) publicly proposes for notice and comment or otherwise promulgates a new regulation, *it shall identify at least two existing regulations to be repealed.*

(b) For fiscal year 2017, which is in progress, the heads of all agencies are directed that *the total incremental cost of all new regulations, including repealed regulations, to be finalized this year shall be no greater than zero,* unless otherwise required by law or consistent with advice provided in writing by the Director of the Office of Management and Budget (Director).

In the administration's Unified Agenda of Regulatory and Deregulatory Actions, it identifies 1,579 delayed or withdrawn actions. Of these, 635 regulations were withdrawn, 244 regulations were delayed, and 700 were suspended or otherwise prorogued.

Some of the most salutary rollbacks are:

➤ End of "Sue & Settle" – Ever wonder how left-wing agitprop groups get so much money? Part of the explanation is that leftists give to these groups the way Christians tithe to their churches. But the other reason is the shakedown scheme known as "sue and settle." This destructive practice involved an unholy alliance between leftist advocacy groups and the Executive Branch. The advocacy group would sue a corporation under the jurisdiction of some federal regulatory body. The regulator or enforcement agency (often the EPA or Department of Justice) would actively conspire with the plaintiff to squeeze a hefty monetary settlement and some regulatory concession out of the defendant, with the settlement going to the plaintiff. The plaintiff gets the money and the Feds get more power. The EPA's Scott Pruitt and Attorney General Jeff Sessions both announced that they would abandon this practice.

➢ Reporting Reduction – The Trump administration stayed an Obama-era rule "that would have required businesses with 100 or more employees to report on what they pay employees by job category, sex, race, and ethnicity."

➢ The Clean Water Act / Waters of the United States – The Clean Water Act has long been used as a pretext for violating property rights and stifling development. The Obama administration proposed a much expanded definition of the "waters of the United States" which would include not just major navigable waterways and wetlands but basically everything damper than a saltine cracker. The EPA and the Army Corps of Engineers issued a joint statement delaying implementation of the new definition for two years, during which they time they will work on a revision. This is a stay-of-execution that should turn into a commutation. But that will require action by Congress.

The American people have dodged a bullet, actually a veritable hail of gunfire, but the shooter is still armed and dangerous. He must be disarmed and rendered harmless.

➤ Repeal of the Clean Power Plan – The EPA has been the tip of the spear for much government overreach in recent years, powered by virtually limitless rulemaking authority and religious fervor attached to climate alarmism. Obama's Clean Power Plan was really a power grab. The Heritage Foundation described it as "the centerpiece of the Obama administration's global warming crusade." The Environmental Protection Agency on October 16, 2017, published its proposed repeal of the regulation on the grounds that the rulemaking exceeded the agency's statutory authority. Repealing this rule will save $33 billion.

➤ Regulatory Flexibility for Retailers in the Supplemental Nutrition Assistance Program (SNAP) – The government abstract says it best: "This rule provides additional flexibilities to retailers applying to participate in SNAP as authorized food stores. The Agricultural Act of 2014 amended the Food and Nutrition Act of 2008 to increase the requirement that certain Supplemental Nutrition Assistance Program (SNAP) authorized retail food stores have available on a continuous basis at least three varieties of items in each of four staple food categories, to a mandatory minimum of seven varieties. The Food and Nutrition Service (FNS) codified these mandatory requirements. This change will provide retailers with more flexibility in meeting the variety standards of the enhanced SNAP eligibility requirements."

THE CONGRESSIONAL REVIEW ACT'S SUBTLE POWER

In 2017, Congress repealed fifteen regulations using the Congressional Review Act. Passed by the Republican Congress in 1996 and signed into law by Bill Clinton, the CRA gives Congress the power to review and overrule new regulations within sixty days of their promulgation by means of a joint resolution. Because it requires action by both houses of Congress and the president, the CRA is, by nature, most likely come into play only after the party in power changes. So we can't expect any CRA actions in the future, but we can nonetheless rejoice over the victories already won. Some of the most noteworthy include:

> The nullification of a rule allowing class action lawsuits against banks and credit card companies to resolve financial disputes. On July 19, 2017, the Consumer Financial Protection Bureau (CFPB) issued a final rule banning certain financial companies from using mandatory arbitration clauses in consumer contracts, including checking account and credit card contracts. The rule was supposed to provide the opportunity for alternative legal recourse for harmed consumers against these financial companies, most importantly class action lawsuits. Financial companies and the Treasury Department claimed that the CFPB's own analysis demonstrated the rule's ineffectiveness and that the rule primarily benefitted trial lawyers. Consumer advocates and congressional Democrats supported

the rule. The day after the final rule was published, Rep. Keith Rothfus (R-PA) introduced a joint resolution of disapproval to nullify the rule under the Congressional Review Act. Five days later, the resolution passed the House, with votes along party lines. Senate Democrats staged a series of high-visibility press conferences in support of the rule, focusing on recent prominent issues at Wells Fargo and Equifax. On October 24, 2017, the resolution narrowly passed the Senate, 51–50, with the vice president breaking the tie after two Republicans voted against it. On November 1, 2017, the resolution was signed by President Trump and became law, nullifying the rule.

➤ The reform of Title X Family Planning Program allows states to block Planned Parenthood from receiving funding under the Title X program. Congress may not have been able to defund the nation's largest chain of abortion clinics, but it at least passed HJ 43, which reformed an Obama-era rule and struck a blow for federalism by handing power back to the states.

> The Department of the Interior's Stream Protection Rule could have destroyed one-third of all U.S. coal mining jobs had it been implemented. It was one of the first regulations repealed under the CRA, prompting *The Huffington Post* to screech, "Donald Trump's Assault on Clean Water Laws Has Already Begun." We'll call their consternation a no-cost bonus.

> The repeal of the Elizabeth Warren–inspired Consumer Finance Protection Board's noxious anti-arbitration rule was signed by President Trump in November 2017. The rule disallowed standard arbitration language in everyday agreements governing everything from credit cards to car loans to bank accounts. If implemented, it would have permitted lawsuits

for every niggling dispute and would have effectively created a tax payable to trial lawyers who sought to reap billions, a portion of which would have gone to their protectors and enablers in the Democratic Party.

These repeals and rescissions represent big wins for individual liberty. But the apparatus and the appetite to recreate them still exists. To put it another way, the American people have dodged a bullet, actually a veritable hail of gunfire, but the shooter is still armed and dangerous. He must be disarmed and rendered harmless. Congress should act, but probably won't. If not, the president should use his authority to shut down as much of the deep state as possible.

HEALING HEALTHCARE

Ronald Reagan was famous for his memorable quips about government. In that vein he described the progressive view of the economy: "If it moves, tax it. If it keeps moving,

*As you might expect, guidance
that comes from the Feds is not
widely understood to be optional.
Rather, it is an instruction,
a mandate if you will.*

regulate it. And if it stops moving, subsidize it." This ethos has been nowhere more apparent than with healthcare. Obamacare's complex puzzle of taxes, regulations, and subsidies took Reagan's insight to absurd levels.

Enter Dr. Scott Gottlieb, Trump's FDA Administrator. When Gottlieb was nominated in March 2017, the *Los Angeles Times*, among many, many others, lamented the choice and ran a story called, "Farewell to Drug Regulation," referring to Gottlieb as a "bona fide pharma shill." If a man is known by his enemies, this story suggests that Gottlieb was an inspired choice. And he has proven to be.

Rather than being a "bona fide pharma shill," Gottlieb is bringing competition to drugs. The rent-seeking drug manufacturers may not like it, but competition drives down the cost of drugs for patients. Now, the FDA is not simply approving a single generic alternative, but several. When there is a single generic, the generic manufacturer usually reduces the price a bit below that of the name-brand alternative and reaps outsized profits in the process. By approving multiple generics of the same drug, the FDA creates an environment where prices drop meaningfully owing to real competition. To this end, Bloomberg reports that "the FDA also wants to prioritize applications for medicines when there are fewer than three competing generic options."

In 2017, the FDA saw "record generic-drug approvals and a multi-year high in novel drug approvals, while also working to speed more medical devices to market. [Gottlieb's] agency has suggested it might be more flexible in approving drugs and will try to get cancer drugs to market more quickly, using data from smaller and faster clinical trials." The 763 generic approvals in 2017 set the stage for even more in 2018, and for a regulatory regime that supports the sort of innovation and competition that once made American healthcare both excellent and affordable.

Gottlieb also pushed through rules that will foster innovation in the development of medical devices, including new guidance for the quick approval of devices not already covered under the FDA's Fast Track approval guidelines. The move was cheered by doctors and device companies. When implemented, it will mean that they can get new products to market years faster, and at a much lower cost.

What a difference an election makes. Under Obamacare, medical devices – those life-saving or improving technologies like cardiac stents, replacement knees, and surgical implements – were subject to a special tax. If you want less of something, tax it. That was how Obama & Co. approached healthcare: the most expensive free care you couldn't get.

If you want less of something, tax it.

Often overlooked in discussions of the size of government is the actual size of government. It's huge. Private industry has used technology to be more efficient, that is to say, it can produce more with less labor. When it comes to the federal government, the opposite is true. Of course, the federal government should be doing fewer things. But those things which it must do, it should do better. That's why President Trump started his tenure in office with a federal hiring freeze that began on January 23. It lasted for 73 days before the OMB Director Mick Mulvaney ended it and asked for each Department, Agency, Commission, Administration, and other federal fiefdom to submit a reorganization plan for Fiscal Year 2019 and beyond.

Mulvaney has been an unsung hero in the never-ending fight to shrink Leviathan. And when I say shrink, I adhere to the conventional definition, "to become or make smaller," not the Washington definition: "grow ever so slightly more slowly than last year." The budget guidance Mulvaney gave all federal agencies in April 2017 directed them to reduce their footprint. It was a one-day story; the political media quickly descended into tabloid melodrama about Russia. Remember, this was just weeks after President Trump claimed in a tweet that his campaign had been wiretapped. Thanks to Representative Devin Nunes, we now know that the President was correct. While political reporters were still hyperventilating over Trump's claim, Mulvaney was pursuing a policy to reduce the size of government.

Final proposals were due to Mulvaney by September 30, but by the end of July 2017 the federal government had already shed 11,000 jobs, reversing a trend shared by Presidents Bush and Obama, who had both increased the federal workforce immediately upon assuming office. During this initial period of downsizing, it was reported that "some agencies [were] already using separation incentives to push employees out the door. Trump's fiscal 2018 blueprint called for a net reduction of only 1,000 civil servants, as job losses at most agencies were set to be mostly offset by gains at the Defense, Homeland Security and Veterans Affairs departments."

In the actual case, federal employment declined sharply between February 2017 and February 2018, going from 2.183 million to

---

The Trump administration would do well to remember the old adage that one should always govern as if he will soon be out of power. Legislation is durable; executive action is not.

2.172 million. This recalls to mind the old joke about what you call 1,000 lawyers at the bottom of the ocean: a good start.

Many agencies and departments have

proposed shrinking their workforces by attrition, early retirements, and buyouts. Among these are the Departments of Education, Interior, Justice, and State. Only the Department of Agriculture, with its 87,000 employees, and headed by Sonny Perdue, submitted a plan that declined to reduce its workforce at all. Who knew that the Department of Agriculture, alone among federal bureaucracies, was so efficiently run that it could not shed a single employee without jeopardizing its mission of doling out farm subsidies and food stamps?

President Trump has already demonstrated that shrinking government, that is to say, actually reducing the headcount, can be done. He is, after all, famous for saying, "You're fired!" on his television show. It's past time to expand on that theme. Reorganization and efficient management of fundamentally flawed enterprises offers a palliative when the cure is already well known.

President Trump should propose legislation to Congress to shutter the Departments of Commerce, Education, and Energy, and to consolidate and shrink others. While Congress considers (Washington pronunciation: dithers), Trump should use the authority he has to buy out or give early retirement to all non-political employees in those Departments and other non-essential agencies. It shouldn't be hard to find a few willing takers.

One interesting target is the State Department. It is, perhaps, the center of the deep state. It's been so bad for so long that Senator Jesse Helms once quipped that he hoped the State Department would open an American desk. After World War II, it became a de facto colonial office intent on running the world – with or without the approval of Congress or the president. That must stop, and the only way to do it is to fire its employees. All of them. Just as American commerce would continue in the absence of the Department of Commerce and education would continue without the Department of Education, America's relations with foreign powers would continue without the State Department. In fact, they would probably improve as we recovered the view that served the country so well for so long, summed up nicely by President John Quincy Adams, who warned that "She [America] well knows that by once enlisting under other banners than her own, were they even the banners of foreign independence, she would involve herself beyond the power of extrication, in all the wars of interest and intrigue, of individual avarice, envy, and ambition, which assume the colors and usurp the standard of freedom. The fundamental maxims of her policy would insensibly change from *liberty* to *force*.... She might become the dictatress of the world. She would be no longer the ruler of her own spirit."

A DEAR JOHN LETTER FOR DEAR COLLEAGUE LETTERS

In 2011 Obama's Department of Education turned the already infamous Title IX into a powerful weapon in the Left's war on men, a war being waged most vigorously and with the least regard for the rule of law on college campuses. Title IX is that obscure section of federal law that has been used to mandate the funding of money-losing women's specialty sports at the nation's colleges and universities at the expense of money-making men's sports. Using Title IX as a pretext, the Obama administration issued a "Dear Colleague Letter" to the nation's college administrators. This letter provided "guidance" for the appropriate handling and adjudication of sexual assault and harassment claims in university "courts."

As you might expect, guidance that comes from the Feds is not widely understood to be optional. Rather, it is an instruction, a mandate if you will. The original 2011 letter was expanded and clarified in a subsequent letter – providing additional "guidance" – in 2014. The practical effect was to create kangaroo courts that deprive the accused of the usual rights afforded a defendant and to dramatically lower the burden of proof. The Reason Foundation described it this way:

> *The previous guidance chipped away at due process in several ways. It lowered the burden of proof to a "preponderance of the evidence" standard, which meant that accused students could be found responsible for sexual misconduct if administrators were only 51 percent convinced of the charges; it discouraged allowing the accused and accuser to cross-examine each other, reasoning that this could prove traumatizing for survivors of rape; and it stipulated that accusers should have the right to appeal contrary rulings, allowing accused students to be re-tried even after they had been judged innocent.*

The authors of *The Campus Rape Frenzy*, K C Johnson and Stuart Taylor, Jr., estimate that compliance costs exceeded $1 billion per year. This pales in comparison to the cost in human suffering – the lives ruined and reputations lost. Remember the Duke lacrosse case that saw the university's lacrosse team exonerated and the politically minded prosecutor convicted of numerous abuses, which led to him being removed from office, disbarred, and sent to prison? That was just one high-profile example of a scenario played out repeatedly across the country and empowered and encouraged – nearly mandated – by the "guidance" from Obama's Department of Education.

As Reagan's falsely maligned Secretary of Labor rightly complained after being the subject of false accusations repeated endlessly by an anti-Republican press (sound familiar?), "Where do I go to get my reputation back?"

In September 2017, Trump's Education Secretary, Betsy DeVos, rescinded the Obama-era rules. Colleges and universities are now free to return to the *status quo ante* and to basic rules of fair play for the accused. Significantly, they are not required to do so, though DeVos is formulating a replacement policy. This is a major win for President Trump, the American people, and most of all for decency. But much additional work remains to be done to improve the situation on campuses – especially when it comes to free speech, which is under a sustained attack from the Left, who repeatedly use the word "tolerance" while practicing insidious intolerance.

SIGNS OF LIFE IN CONGRESS

Much of the work in shrinking Leviathan to date has been done by the executive branch. But after tasting success with the tax reform bill, and inspired by the president's example, Congress is taking some small steps in the right direction. In March 2018 the Senate passed legislation with broad support in the House for reducing regulations and limitations placed on small and mid-sized banks in the wake of the 2008 financial crisis. The legislation even gained eighteen red-state Democrats in the process. The *Wall Street Journal* described it this way:

A core piece of the Senate bill could cut to 12 from 38 the number of banks subject to heightened Federal Reserve oversight by raising a key regulatory threshold to $250 billion in assets from the current $50 billion. The Fed has already eased stress tests for midsize banks, but Dodd-Frank limits the Fed's reach because it spells out that all banks above $50 billion in assets must face stricter rules. By effectively raising that threshold to $250 billion, the new legislation could give regulators more space to lighten the load....

Another provision — a flashpoint in the debate over the bill — would exclude banks that originate fewer than 500 mortgages annually from having to report certain racial and income data on their mortgages, unless they perform poorly on tests of lending discrimination.

Critics charge the provision could make it tougher to police racial discrimination in lending, though supporters deny the charge. They point to a Fed Bank of Kansas City analysis that found only about 3.5% of total reportable data will be lost, while roughly 75% of banks will receive relief under the provision.

Stacey Tronson, the compliance officer for Cornerstone Bank, a North Dakota bank with 14 locations, said the compliance costs for the mortgage-reporting requirements alone have led

other banks in her state to exit from the mort-
gage lending business altogether. "No small bank
can continue to weather that," she said.

Undoing regulations made in the wake of, and as a reaction to, the financial crisis is a good place for Congress to start in its quest to restore power to the people. As Senator Mike Crapo (R-ID) explained, "This bill has received widespread support for good reason: the cycle of lending and job creation has been stifled by onerous regulation."

There is more to be done. Again, reducing regulation is helpful, but temporary. Elimination of the underpinnings of the deep state itself is essential for victory. Interestingly, President Trump addressed this issue in part when he presented six principles that will guide his forthcoming infrastructure proposal. The third and fourth of those principles bear directly on his larger mission to reduce the size of the federal government and return power back either to states and municipalities or to the people themselves. These principles should guide Congress not just as it considers the infrastructure plan, but in everything it does.

The notable principles are:

➤ Decision making authority will be returned to State and local governments.

➤ Regulatory barriers that needlessly get in the way of infrastructure projects will be removed.

The President's plan for doing so includes streamlining permitting and approval processes, returning significant regulatory power back to the states, and rationalizing and reforming licensing requirements for individuals seeking work on infrastructure projects. Remember Obama's "shovel-ready projects" when he was selling the budget-busting stimulus bill in 2009? Not only were the projects not shovel-ready (indeed, many were not yet a gleam in a crony-capitalist's eye), when they were conceived many were slowed down by layers of subsidiary regulation including licensing requirements that kept people from gainful employment. Not to worry though, Obama was also expanding access to food stamps and Obamaphones at the same time!

Yet these principles described by the president have a broader application and a more significant constitutional mandate than just infrastructure. In particular, the third principle is essential: return power to state and local government. These authorities are closer to the problems they purport to solve, are more responsive, and are more likely to allow people maximum autonomy.

Demilitarizing & Disarming the Deep State

The militarization of the deep state should be the focus of swift action. Conservatives raised the issue occasionally during the Obama years but must use the power they have now to deescalate a situation that is ripe for abuse and that can only grow worse over time. There are currently at least 44 non–law enforcement agencies that have their own heavily armed police forces. These are agencies, bureaus, and departments like the IRS, the EPA, the Department of Education, the Small Business Administration, and the National Oceanic and Atmospheric Administration. Even the Smithsonian has its own police force.

Most of these new private police forces came into being under a little known or remarked upon provision in the 2002 Homeland Security Act.

The relevant section provides that these agencies, under the auspices of their internal Inspector Generals, may:

(*A*) carry a firearm *while engaged in official duties as authorized under this Act or other statute, or as expressly authorized by the Attorney General;* (*B*) make an arrest without a warrant *while engaged in official duties as authorized under this Act or other statute, or as expressly authorized by the Attorney General, for any offense against the United States committed in the presence of such Inspector General, Assistant Inspector General, or agent, or for any felony cognizable under the laws of the United*

States if such Inspector General, Assistant Inspector General, or agent has reasonable grounds to believe that the person to be arrested has committed or is committing such felony; and (C) seek and execute warrants for arrest, search of a premises, or seizure of evidence issued under the authority of the United States *upon probable cause to believe that a violation has been committed.*

The power to deprive people of their lives and property – to participate in the state's monopoly on violence – should be handled with great care. Instead, it has been given away willy-nilly so that every petty bureaucratic chieftain becomes a warlord.

Abuse of such unchecked power should be expected. It has already led to egregious violations of people's rights including harassment and intimidation in their homes. For example:

➤ In 2003, six agents arrayed in tactical gear like a SWAT team raided the home of a sixty-year-old grandmother, Kathy Norris, for the crimes of incomplete paperwork in the importation of orchids. Her husband, George Norris, spent two years in prison for his crimes.

- ➤ FDA agents raided the Rainbow Acres Amish farm for selling unpasteurized milk to customers who wanted raw milk.

- ➤ In 2011, Department of Education agents in full tactical gear conducted a pre-dawn raid on the home of Kenneth Wright, handcuffing him, ransacking the house, and terrorizing his three small children. The alleged crime? Wright's estranged wife, who did not live in the house, was suspected of misusing federal aid for students – a run-of-the-mill financial crime which did not even involve Wright himself.

There have been no such abuses under the Trump administration, mostly because Trump appointees, far from being the budding tyrants portrayed in the mainstream media, are protective of citizens' right to security in their person and their property, and demonstrate an appropriate circumspection regarding the use of police power. But this approach can change with a change in administrations. At a minimum, Trump should reverse the offending provision of the Homeland Security Act, disarm the bureaucrats via executive order, and ask Congress to ratify the move with legislation that he signs.

There is much Donald Trump can do unilaterally using executive power. But there are many areas where Congress must act. The body has been relatively diligent in applying the Congressional Review Act, but remains timid when it comes to asserting its power as a separate, co-equal branch of government and the one closest to the people and with the power to legislate. Demilitarizing the bureaucracy can and should be done by executive order. But the Trump administration would do well to remember the old adage that one should always govern as if he will soon be out of power. Legislation is durable; executive action is not. The disarmament of the administrative state is better done by Congress so that a future president does not re-arm the EPA, to take one chilling example.

THE RETURN OF AMERICAN AUTONOMY

The task of returning autonomy to the American people is of the utmost importance. It is essential if we wish to regain our natural and historic liberties and avoid the depredations of a leviathan state which will consume the whole of society if left unchecked.

Nick Land explained the modern peril this way:

Somewhere before Jerusalem is reached, the inarticulate pluralism of a free society has been transformed into the assertive multiculturalism of a soft-totalitarian democracy.

The Jews of 17th-century Amsterdam, or the Huguenots of 18th-century London, enjoyed the right to be left alone, and enriched their host societies in return. The democratically-empowered grievance groups of later modern times are incited by political leaders to demand a (fundamentally illiberal) right to be heard, with social consequences that are predominantly malignant. For politicians, however, who iden-tify and promote themselves as the voice of the unheard and the ignored, the self-interest at stake could hardly be more obvious.

Tolerance, which once presupposed neglect, now decries it, and in so doing becomes its opposite.

America has historically been a middle-class commercial republic sustained by a self-sufficient citizenry. The growth of the state not only impinges on the rights and prerogatives of the American people, it creates a set of perverse incentives and restrictions that render Americans' very independence – supposedly something *protected* by the state – impossible.

President Trump deserves credit both for recognizing the problem and for using his authority to reverse some of the worst excesses of the Obama administration. But even these actions only return the country to where it was in 2008. Unfortunately, the apparatus remains in place so that a future president – be it a Democrat or a Republican – can restart the expansion of government power. The next frontier is dismantling the apparatus and returning sovereignty to the American people.

First American edition published in 2018 by Encounter Books, an activity of Encounter for Culture and Education, Inc., a nonprofit, tax exempt corporation. Encounter Books website address: www.encounterbooks.com

Manufactured in the United States and printed on acid-free paper. The paper used in this publication meets the minimum requirements of ANSI / NISO Z39.48–1992 (R 1997) (*Permanence of Paper*).

FIRST AMERICAN EDITION

LIBRARY OF CONGRESS CATALOGING-IN-PUBLICATION DATA IS AVAILABLE

Buskirk, Chris
Trump vs. the leviathan / Chris Buskirk.
pages   cm. — (Encounter broadsides ; 57)
ISBN 978-1-64177-031-6 (pbk. : alk. paper) —
ISBN 978-1-64177-032-3 (ebook)

10 9 8 7 6 5 4 3 2 1